TO EVERYTHING THERE IS A SEASON, AND A TIME TO EVERY PURPOSE UNDER THE HEAVEN;

A time to be born, and a time to die;
A time to plant, and a time to pluck up that which is planted;
A time to kill, and a time to heal;
A time to break down, and a time to build up;
A time to weep, and a time to laugh;
A time to mourn, and a time to dance;
A time to cast away stones, and a time to gather stones together;
A time to embrace, and a time to refrain from embracing;
A time to get, and a time to lose;
A time to keep, and a time to cast away;
A time to rend, and a time to sew;
A time to keep silence, and a time to speak;
A time to love, and a time to hate;
A time of war, and a time of peace.

-ECCLESIASTES 3:1-8

Grace FULL Seasons: Stories of Triumph, Victory and God's Faithfulness Through The Seasons of Life

Copyright 2020 by Debrayta Salley Enterprises L.L.C. All rights reserved.

No part of this publication may be reproduced, stored in a retrieval system or transmitted in any way by any means, electronic, mechanical, photocopy, recording or otherwise without the prior permission of the author (s) except as provided by USA copyright law. Thank you for acknowledging and supporting the authors' rights.

Published by Debrayta Salley Enterprises, L.L.C.
Baltimore, Maryland 21244

www.deelifmentor.com

Cover & Layout Design
Type A Designs – Allycia Dickens |Designer
https://typeadesigns.com

Published in the United States of America

ISBN for paperback: 978-0-578-57495-0

AUTHOR ACKNOWLEDGMENTS

Author Denise Madden

First, I would like to thank our Lord and Savior Jesus Christ for giving me the strength to withstand the test and trials faced along my journey. I would also like to thank my Mom who is very loving and supportive of my endeavors. Lastly, I thank, Love, and appreciate my amazing kids, London, Maci, and Jadon, and my grandson Collin. They are my motivation for everything that I do. My prayer is that what I have endured will help someone else along their journey. Thanks, and God Bless.

Author Dawn Courtney Mason

My dear Rev, Mia, and Nehemiah, thank you for encouraging, inspiring, and enlightening me. This work starts at home. I love you.

Thank you! My dear village for allowing me to share my thoughts and supporting what I am inspired to do.

Thank you so much Ms. Debrayta "Dee" Salley for seeing the vision and sharing this endeavor with us all. It has been a pleasure working with you. Sometimes the greatest challenge is not facing the world, but looking at yourself in the mirror. It shows you all the joy and pain you have endured through the years. I faced that woman in the mirror and challenged her to share from her heart the story you will read about me.

I am Diligent, Aware, Wise, and Necessary. I am DAWN.

Peace Love Blessings abundantly always
"Behold, we count them happy which endure." James 5:11

Author Mitzi Carrasquillo

Thank you to my Lord and Savior Jesus Christ. I would not be here without Your love for me, this opportunity would not be possible without You. Thank you, Lord, for assigning Debrayta Salley with this book and her obedience to bring it to fruition to bless Your Kingdom.

To my husband and love of my life for 32 years, Jose Carrasquillo, thank you for your unselfish, unwavering and unconditional love and support for this assignment God has set upon us. MY ROCK! I love you.

I'm truly blessed and honored to be the mother to Jeanee and Stephan Franklin, Jazmine and Malcolm Hall and Jose Carrasquillo III. My children are everything to me!! They are the essence of my Lord and Savior's love, healing and restoration for me, and the reason my heart beats each day. To my adorable "grand-kisses" who bring me such overwhelming joy with a refreshed, renewed dose of special love, I love you with all my heart Xavier, Sean, Justice and Leilani.

I would not be the strong woman of God that I am without those who loved me the most as their daughter, my parents, Jesse Jr. and Jean Spencer. Thank you for this imperfect, but precious life. I love you dearly!!!

Love and blessings to each of my siblings, the Spencer, Carrasquillo and Cintron Family. To my church family, Jubilee Christian Church and Victory Christian Church International, I'm thankful to serve alongside you, simply thank you.

Alishia Louis-Potter, thank you for your gift of sister love and intercessory prayer on 8/29/17. My chapter title is what you sowed into me. God bless you and thank you sis!

I dedicate my presence in this book to my sidekick, my girl and loving mother, Jean, my handsome, baby brother, Damien and to the sweetest mother-in-love, Hortencia Lopez. May you continue to rest in God's perfect peace.

Author Mae Golden

First, I thank God, Jesus and the Holy Spirit. Through God, all of this has been made possible. Through Jesus, I have salvation that I am constantly thankful to have. Through the Holy Spirit, I am learning the importance of patience in my own process, how to love others in their process and the significance of being Spirit-led.

I thank my parents for the life they gave me and how they did the best that they could with what they had and knew. Regardless of all I've been through, I developed resilience to whatever life brings. All of it has helped to make me the woman that I am; warts and all. Lol! I've never went to bed hungry nor homeless; that's saying plenty!

I thank my husband and my children. I have learned loads about life while traveling around the country for his work and raising our children. Both of them supplied me many laughs and showed me how to appreciate the little things in life.

I thank my female posse, who I call "Warrior Women." They know who they are. For me, they are part of my landline to the God when I am having a meltdown about life. They listen. They give it to me straight when needed. But before and after they do any of that…they Pray. Lastly, but certainly not least, I thank Debrayta Salley. When she asked me about participating in this project, I had to think (and pray hard) multiple times before saying yes. Dee has been a constant cheerleader for any endeavor I've attempted. She's the friend who sees possibility (and the plan to make it happen) when I tell her what I'm thinking. She doesn't blow smoke, though. We all need at least a friend or two who helps us dream that dream, before they help us see the roadblocks, because let's face it, dreaming is fun (and necessary)! Plus, she pulled together all of us to work on a project and most of us don't even know each other. Now, what does that say about her leadership?!!!

Author Lena Dennis

First and foremost, I must give God all the Praise and Glory for His Grace and Mercy that has allowed me to be here for such a time as this. I give Him thanks for keeping me, cleaning me up and freeing me for His use.

To my parents, the late Leroy Evans and Mary Martin, thank you for letting God use you as the vessels to birth me. A special Thank you to Bruce Owen Dennis, Jr. my amazing husband who first planted the seeds to help me in my journey and stayed the course with me even when I was running rampant and living quite messy life.

Debrayta Salley, thank you for your obedience in following the vision/dream that was placed in your spirit to compile this book project. May you continue to keep your ear inclined to God's heart to hear and know His voice so that you can continue to be a catalyst to empower, encourage, and inform others that they matter and their lives are not in vain.

Author Debrayta Salley

First and foremost, I would like to give Thanks and Praise to my Heavenly Father who was with me when I was in my wilderness season. He has truly never left or forsaken me. He has always been there loving me and holding me close, despite my condition or state of mind.

To every Leader who has had a hand in my Spiritual Development, has trusted me to serve in your Ministry, allowed me to stand behind your Pulpit, spoke into my life, supported the God in me, or pushed me to another level in God – Thank You! Some of you planted seeds and some of you watered them through your prayers and guidance. God is continuing the growth process for the work that has begun. Regardless of the length of time I served in Ministry alongside you, please know that it was not in vain.

To my dear son, Jordan Salley, I am so proud of the Young Man of God that you are becoming. God's Hand was on your life before you were even conceived in the womb. We have walked through many difficult life seasons and it has not turned you away from desiring to know and serve our Lord and Savior, Jesus Christ. I pray that God will continue to lead you to seek and know Him for yourself. Always remember that nothing in Life is worth more than your personal relationship with Jesus Christ.

To my small group of Praying Friends. Thank you for all of your prayers and always giving me your opinion, but not from a place of judgment. Thank you for the heartfelt conversations, tons of laughs, and spontaneous outings/meals or seafood fest. I appreciate you all!

Last but not least, Thank you to the Ladies of the *Grace FULL Seasons Anthology*. First for trusting me with your stories. Secondly, for making the creative process drama free and most of all, for your bravery in stepping out and telling your stories. I am so excited for you and so honored to have been Blessed with the opportunity to support you through this project.

A special Thank you to Allycia Dickens of Type A Designs. Thank you so much for all of your assistance with this project. This project could not have been completed without your Graphic, Design and Editing expertise. May God Continue to Bless and Prosper your Business.

INTRODUCTION

Let us therefore come Boldly to the Throne of Grace with confidence, so that we may receive Mercy, and find Grace to help us in our time of need.
- Hebrews 4:16

Grace is defined as: *A simple elegance or refinement of movement.* In Biblical terms, it is also a gift from our Heavenly Father given through His Son, Jesus Christ. In scripture, the word Grace refers to "the enabling power and spiritual healing offered through the mercy and love of Jesus Christ."

Seasons consist of: Winter, Spring, Summer and Fall. These represent the four divisions of the year. Each season is marked by particular weather patterns and daylight hours which result from the Earth's changing position with the Sun. Similarly, in life, we each journey through times that are chilly, cold, stormy, windy, etc. but because trouble can never last always, eventually, our seasons change over to full sunny days, beautiful flowers, and clear, blue skies.

Within the pages of this book, you will find testimonies of Triumph, Victory, and God's Faithfulness through the Seasons of Life from six Women of Faith. These women have stepped boldly out of their comfort zones to share stories of: deliverance from substance abuse, healing from divorce, learning to laugh again after losing their smile, breaking free from hurt and anger from childhood experiences, finding purpose in pain and discovering how to make choices that are divinely-led and inspired.

Truly, it was God's Grace that gave each of these women the Faith and Strength to press through the stormy-weather seasons so that they would reach the bright and sunny days. These times were not without pain, disappointment, or frustration; but in the end, the wisdom gained and the inspiration gleaned for the pouring out into the lives of someone else makes it all worthwhile. More importantly, because God never left their side, it brought them each closer to the One who carries us through the Seasons of Life – Our Lord and Savior Jesus Christ. When we are able to see Him in it and turn over the wheel to Him along the ride of our journeys, He truly does work EVERYTHING together for our GOOD!

It's been a pleasure for me to read and compile the stories of these courageous women! I pray that every reader is blessed and impacted by their transparency. Enjoy and be sure to reach out to the authors especially if their stories speak loudly to your spirit.

Debrayta Salley
Author, Visionary/Compiler of the *Grace FULL Seasons Anthology*

TABLE OF CONTENTS

CHAPTER 1
My Time to Laugh and Shine
Author: Dawn Courtney Mason

CHAPTER 2
Rebuilding on Clear Land
Author: Debrayta D. Salley

CHAPTER 3
I Had to Die to Myself so I could LIVE AGAIN
Author: Lena Dennis

CHAPTER 4
No Longer Broken
A transparent and inspirational look at the life of a Godly Mother, Gigi, Counselor, Educator and Mentor
Author: Denise Madden

CHAPTER 5
A Plan Behind the Pain
Author: Mitzi L. Carrasquillo

CHAPTER 6
My Father's Daughter
Author: Mae Golden

MY TIME TO LAUGH AND SHINE

Author: Dawn Courtney Mason

Ecclesiastes 3:1,4

"For everything there is a season, for every matter under heaven: [4a] time to weep, and a time to laugh."

Ecclesiastes 3:1,4 (English Standard Version)

Good morning Lord, I had the most interesting dream last night. I stood up for myself to those who tried to be mean to me. It was empowering. Help me to use my influence for good. Continue to develop my gifts; so, I can be of better use to you, Lord, my husband, my children, my church, my community, and my world. Help me to be bold and courageous. -July 4, 2017, Journal entry

Good morning Lord, it's Dawn. Thank you for the miracles big and small that I have been experiencing. Forgive me for not always trusting you and believing that you would stand for me. I give my life back to you. Help me to be better not bitter. In Jesus' name, Amen.
-January 15, 2015, Journal entry

My journal entries for the day. One with a big heart yet has shared many tears over the years. That is me. My heart has been like an open book on display for only those close to me to see, but somehow now the world.

I once was told that I had the gift of loving unconditionally, and I do. The Lord specifically told me that I had to love those who have hurt me in spite of their transgressions. Imagine that. Funny, God must really trust me, but I have been told that, too. He trusts me.

It has been my prayer forever that I be a wise and knowledgeable woman. I figured that if I possess these qualities then, decision-making would come easy. I can tell you that is not so. Let the truth be told, I have not had a bad life. I have had a few bumps and bruises along the way. What good Christian girl does not want to fit in with crowd? Surely, I wanted people to like me.

My life began in a small community in Virginia, where I grew up with my maternal grandparents Pauline and Louis Courtney. My grandmother was graceful, stylish, and wise. Granddaddy was handsome, stylish, and also very wise. I am still learning from them, even today.

It was after I was married and had my first child that I would learn why I came to live with them. During a visit with him in conversation, my granddad shared with me that it was my grandmother, who had brought me home from the hospital.

Making the decision to allow my grandparents to raise me had to have been difficult for my parents, but they were both young and just out of high school at the time. Although my parents never made me feel unwanted, there are just some realities one cannot grasp as a child. In fact, my dad told me that I was the best birthday gift he received that year. My birthday just happened to be the day after his. I still felt unwanted and out-of-place.

My parents and sister lived in another state; so, my access to them was only during school breaks and holidays. When I think about it, there are days even now when I struggle with feelings of rejection and wanting to be accepted. But in retrospect, I do believe that I had the childhood I needed to grow.

I was so very close to my grandmother. She was my mentor and best friend. As wise as she was, I, of course, did not always listen to her. She would say things like *"You are free until you are foolish"* or *"Sometimes we do not use the sense God gave us; so, we have to go out and buy some."* "*Your enemies may not harm you, but your best friend will.*" The actions of those you do love can hurt because you care about what they think, say, and do in regards to you. Girls like me wanted to be liked especially by boys. Don't get me wrong, I was liked by boys, but not the same as other girls who seemed more popular.

What was wrong with me? I am cute, smart, and very ambitious. So, what is the problem? I was told by a friend that guys don't like girls like me and what type of girl is that I asked? "*Smart,*" he replied. What a blow to my self-esteem. Needless to say, I did not date much in school and the relationships I did have did not amount to much. It wasn't them; it was me. I had taken on the attitude that I did not really need them anyway. I had a 10-year plan for my life. I was going to go off to college, get a great job as an attorney, get married, and have children. It would be years before I got my family.

I went off to college and I dated. I took my Christian beliefs and values seriously, but I found myself compromising just to be liked. Again, I was cute, smart, and ambitious. I learned really quick that you should not let anyone into to your heart that does not deserve to be to be there. Let's just say that I had run-ins with individuals who did not have my best interest in mind and were more concerned about how they could use me for their benefits. I have never been a wild person, but I wanted to be liked even loved.

Painful lessons you learn when you do not listen to Godly wisdom, but I was grown and wanted to do things my way. *Where was God in my life?* He was there but being ignored by me. What are the choices? Being alone or being around people you know aren't good for you. When they are gone, you feel empty and used. I could not blame anyone except myself. They were just being themselves; I was the one out of place not being who God called me to be.

It is 2001 and I started having unexplainable colon and intestinal issues. Well, the only logical explanation was stress. So, my doctor says to me, "*Find a way to relieve your stress or I am going to medicate you.*" Now, I did not want to be medicated.

One day on the train going to work, a thought came to me; so, I wrote it down. When I got to work, I shared it with some of my co-workers and closest friends. I was still having issues, but I noticed that my writing became a stress-reliever for me. So, I started writing everything that came to thought.

I continued sharing them with my friends and co-workers not just once a week but twice now. The term "Life coaching" was becoming popular and I wanted to explore it for myself. I decided that I would get my certification as a coach.

I found a program operated by one of the most delightful ladies I have ever met. She guided me through the process of being coached and helped me become a certified Life Purpose Coach. I decided I wanted to help; I formed "*It's DAWN*." My mission was to inspire, enlighten, and entertain anyone who wanted to listen to my message.

I was excited and moving forward but then, fear crept in. *Who would want to take coaching from me? I am not famous. As a matter of fact, I had someone question me about my ability to write a book.* The lady's exact words were, "*What makes you qualified to write a book?*" Well, what makes me *not* is how I responded. God is always up to something.

The year 2002 had arrived and one of my good friend's grandmother invited me to her aunt's wedding. It was during the Memorial Day holiday weekend and out of town; so, I decided to go.

I go to the rehearsal dinner with my friend and this nice gentleman sat beside me. He asked me a few questions, and I informed him that I was from out of town just visiting for the wedding. My friend told him that if he was ever in our area, to look us up, and we would cook dinner for him.

The day of the wedding, I would again have a conversation with this nice gentleman. Again, he asked me questions about myself, and we talked about how nice the wedding had been. I even told him that one day his wedding would be equally as nice. I noticed that he was not eating at the reception. So, I asked him why. He had a preaching engagement that evening; he was fasting.

Meanwhile back at the house, the conversation went from how wonderful the wedding festivities were to how this gentleman was looking at me. Grandma said, "*Dawn, that young man is looking for a wife.*" I said, "*What does that have to do with me?*" I was *not* looking for a husband. I had been praying to the Lord about the possibility of a family, but at that time in my life, I had resolved that if I was not married by a certain age, I likely would not ever get married or have children.

A week after I go home, my friend called me excited. She explained to me that she had given him our numbers and he called her. I took his number, and I called him. He called me back and that was the beginning of a new life for me. A few months later, he came to visit me. I met his family that Thanksgiving, and he mine during the Christmas holiday. Time passed, and he moved to Maryland where I was.

We were married on a peaceful day September 2003. By our first wedding anniversary, I was pregnant with our first child, a little girl. She would be born on Thanksgiving Day 2004.

My husband had been telling me that God was calling him back to North

Carolina. *What, please Lord, no*! I knew the Lord was asking him to leave Maryland because ministry was calling him.

Crying all the way, my daughter and I moved with my husband to his hometown in March 2005. The people were nice, but I still felt like a fish out of water. I knew what the Lord was calling him to do, but w*hat about me?* I already had started writing and established It's DAWN, but would my new community accept me? In Maryland, I knew people. I did not know a ton of people and honestly, I wasn't sure that I wanted to. Meeting people was never hard for me; I'm personable.

While my husband was establishing himself in the ministry, I was acclimating myself to my new environment and wanting to fit in. I was hired by the local community college to teach in the workforce development program.

Things were going well then suddenly, I got sick again around April 2006. I went three months without eating anything except applesauce, a baked potato, and ginger ale. I was hospitalized twice and finally diagnosed with Ulcerative Colitis, an autoimmune disorder.

It is not life-threating; however, it can be very debilitating. Again, I had to find a stress-reliever. I started journaling. Two days before my birthday in November 2006, I found out that I was expecting a little boy. He was born July 2007 and I hit the ground running working with a domestic violence organization as their Displaced Homemaker Coordinator. Even though my degree was in Political Science, I found myself using my coaching and writing skills. Soon after, in 2010 my position was terminated. Our family decided to move to another city.

This move brings me to where I am today. Always ministry-minded, my husband started doing outreach work and I again needed something to do. The question has always been: '*Lord what about me?*' The Lord answered me, but not in the way I thought He would. I started working for Livingstone College, and I found my passion – advising students and mentoring them has been so fulfilling.

There have been bumps in the road. My children have seen me go through pain that I thought was unbearable. My son could have only been six years old when he turned to me while watching some music awards program and said, "*Mommy be brave.*"

I knew at that moment I had to be brave for my two children who were depending on me. I have learned that you have to live your own moments. Love is not easy, but it is possible. The rough days make the good days sweeter because you did not give up. Don't expect everything to be perfect because we are imperfect beings. Somedays, you just have to give yourself a breather from the world's cares and enjoy yourself. Keep a cheerful disposition at all times is what my doctor prescribed for me; easier said than done on most days; however, it is doable.

I have had to change my attitude about my life. It is valuable not just for me, but to the individuals I am called to serve.

God has given me the gift to reason and encourage others, but I was not doing anything with it. Again, I was afraid that people would not relate to me. *Who is she and why should I listen to her?*

So, one day, I decided to use my social media platforms to inspire, entertain, and enlighten those individuals willing to come along for the ride. My daily messages are from my heart and are designed to make you think not in particularly of who is conveying the message, but why you think God sent the message to you on that day.

It is a great feeling to receive a message from another part of the world saying that your words are inspiring. I have been asked, "*What is my motivation?*" My *village* is my motivation. I have even been bestowed the title "*Miss America of world peace through daily quotes*" by one of my new readers. I am making my contribution to the world, and it feels so good. Yes, it is my time to laugh. It is my time to shine. Constant self-doubt and low self-esteem did not work well for me. It made me sick; stress will do that to you.

At times, I allowed people who said they loved me to hurt me because I did not stand up for myself out of fear that I would not be liked. My Granddaddy once told me that "*Just because you are born in a ditch, you don't have to stay there.*"

Life happens and every experience is valuable. It is how you look at it and what you do with those experiences is what matters in the grand scheme of things. All I have is my pen and my heart. I let my pen speak for me and as long as I live, I will write.

Dawn Courtney Mason,
the "Miss America of world peace through daily quotes"

Dawn Courtney Mason is a graduate of Howard University, Dawn has a certification in Life Purpose Coaching from *The Success Unlimited Network*® and is the founder of Its DAWN, a multifaceted company focusing on business, lifestyle, and motivation.

Dawn lives her purpose by inspiring others to discover theirs. Committed to her community and helping others, she volunteers with the *Jobs for Life – Salisbury* program.

Dawn is the First Lady of D. M. Ministries where she serves along with her husband. She is happily married to Reverend D. M. Mason and the mother of a lovely daughter, Mia and a handsome son, Nehemiah.

Dawn holds membership in Delta Sigma Theta Sorority, Inc., Delta Psi Epsilon Christian Sorority, Inc., Eta Phi Beta Sorority, Inc., and the National Association of University Women.

CONNECT WITH ME AS FOLLOWS:
EMAIL: itsdawnonline@gmail.com
BLOG: http://itsdawn.wordpress.com
INSTAGRAM: @firstladydawn
FACEBOOK: It's DAWN @itsdawn1
TWITTER: ladaydawn
BUSINESS NUMBER: 704-222-1340

REBUILDING ON CLEAR LAND
A Time to Plant and a Time to Pluck Up that which is Planted
Author: Debrayta D. Salley
Ecclesiastes 3:2

In May 2016, my Memoir, *Back to The Scene of the Crime* was released and it contained my journey through a pattern of low self-esteem, broken relationships, rejection and financial indebtedness, just to name a few. God had brought to my attention a dysfunctional pattern of unhealthy relationships with men.

The external result of my issues had been identified but the root of the problem had not. At that time, I was on a high. After years of hit or miss therapy sessions, self-examination, deep reflection and writing, I was finally able to publish my story; to bring hidden things to light and no longer live in shame or condemnation about unfruitful choices that I had made and life challenges I had endured as a result. But there was more to my story.

Imagine thinking that you have taken sufficient time to process and allow God to heal your wounds only to discover one day that there are more layers of healing that need to be addressed. I quickly learned for myself that Healing is a process.

One year prior, in May 2015, I had made a new vow and commitment to God by laying my flesh down and beginning a lifestyle of celibacy and separation unto Him.

I pressed forward into beginning to know Him more intimately and began steps to walking further into ministry and fulfilling God's assignment on my life. That same month, I joined a very small ministry and dragged my son along with me.

I submitted to the process of further Deliverance and Ministerial Training facilitated by my new Pastor.

Things were going great, or so I thought. We were required to be in church multiple days of the week and late hours into the night. I struggled with remaining obedient to the process, the sacrifice, and how to effectively balance being a Mother, an Employee and a Servant while also managing my health.

I wanted to be all that I could be in all of my roles but the truth of the matter was that I was extremely burnt out, as well as stressed out at work and at home. And I wasn't the only one. My son was acting out in his own way. Not only that, my stress level was at an all-time high.

I quickly came to the conclusion that if I was going to be in good health and productive in anything, I needed to take the time to get real with myself, commit to self-care and seek God for directions on how to move forward. Although this became clear to me six months into my commitment, my desire to accomplish the goal of becoming an Ordained Minister so that my calling would be "official" in Man's sight blinded me from the obvious.

Sometimes we want something so badly that we move ahead of God or out of the path by which He plans to accomplish it. In short, we fail to wait for our Kairos moment or season – "the right, critical, or opportune time."

Similar to the patterns of my past, I failed to count the costs and sincerely seek God before I made the decision. Instead, I made it abruptly and from my emotions instead of under the guidance of Holy Spirit.

I didn't survey the land or take the time to visit and/or be a lay member first before stepping into a Leadership role. I learned a great deal in this servant position and grew in my posture of worship, study and developing a personal relationship with God, but the busyness kept me from seeing that I still had some internal healing to do.

Through this experience, I learned personally that taking on added roles, being excessively busy, and never taking the time to intentionally be still are all Coping Mechanisms when one is avoiding conquering the hard places of life that must ultimately be faced. We all do it – some more than others.

In October 2018, while completing Biblical Life Coach training through *Dream Life Mentors International* (www.dreammentors.org), I learned that this points to our need for Provision, Protection and Acceptance. It also taught me that God doesn't need His children to pursue position, title, or achievement in order to serve others or for Him to use us to fulfill the Mandate that He has assigned to our lives. He's just looking for willing hearts that want to serve.

He certainly didn't need me to make anything happen in my own strength. What He desired was for me to surrender my Heart and Soul fully to Him and Him alone so that the work that He began in me could continue to move forward towards completion.

In essence, Growth and Healing are necessary processes that both take time. It takes us becoming completely undone, naked and unashamed before God and fully submitting to his timeframe – not ours, and certainly not man's.

This takes extreme tunnel vision and the ultimate outcomes should be: (1) Being in the center of God's will and (2) Surrendering to the process of Transformation. Neither of these are for the faint at heart, they require Authenticity and Commitment. As the popular saying goes: "It may not be easy, but it will be worth it."

In October, 2016, I finally surrendered to the still, small voice inside that was telling me to step down from the Minister in Training role and move into an extreme place of self-care/wellness/healing but I didn't know how to effectively communicate that to my Pastor.

Instead, my movement was abrupt and void of a sit-down conversation with my her at that time. Actually, a few months prior, I did have an initial conversation with her and attempted to express my thoughts, heart and what I believed I was hearing from God, but I did not do so in a way that was crystal clear nor was I confident in my delivery. How could I be, when I had doubts myself whether I had actually heard from God clearly. In the end, I allowed man's view to override that of Holy Spirit.

The only thing I knew for sure was that there was a disconnect, something didn't feel right and I needed an intimate and focused period of self-care and Communion with God to get clear. *What kept me from moving forward to accomplish this need?* I couldn't understand it then, but now I know that it was a life-long habit of pleasing others even at the cost of disregarding my desires or needs and therefore, causing harm to myself.

This brings to remembrance the term *"Self-Mutilation"* that Ms. Iyanla Vanzant mentioned during an episode of her show "Fix My Life." This was the first time I had heard the term and its' definition but it was a huge eye opener for me.

Self-Mutilation is definitely the opposite of Self-Care and Self Preservation. It's like "setting yourself on fire to keep others warm." Unfortunately, this is what society portrays as the image of being a Strong Woman.

Listen Ladies, we are called to unselfishly Serve, be a blessing to others and put the needs of others before our own, but never at the expense of directly or indirectly imposing self-harm mentally, spiritually or physically. It's been a long and hard process for me mostly because I had to first come out of denial in order to move towards healing, but I'm finally learning how to make sure that I pour out to others only after I have filled my tank to the rim and overflowing. This has not been easy, but I'm committed to staying the course. I'm also embracing the fact that it is only through maintaining a Lifestyle in God's presence, in His word, and by His Grace, Power and Strength that I could ever be a "Strong" or "Super" Woman. I cling to the fact that - His Strength is made perfect in my weakness. Amen.

Did you know that silence and stillness can be very loud? That's only if we never learn to embrace the silence. I had consistently found this to be my experience but never seemed to be able to reconcile why.

As I have fought to press and journey through my personal healing process the past three years, I have discovered that when we are in a place of quiet and stillness, it causes us to hear our own thoughts, and feel what's lingering deep within our hearts. That's when our Heavenly Father begins to reveal the work that He wants to do in us.

Psalm 46:10 encourages us to:

"Be Still and Know that He is God."

I suspect that God must have foreknew that we would become accustomed to being busy bodies or Martha's if you will. Always going, doing, planning and attending instead of being purposeful while resting in His care – like Mary.

Once again in my life's journey I found myself saying I was going to be still and seek God for the next step, but my actions revealed something different.

I began searching for churches to visit so that my son and I wouldn't be disconnected from the Body of Christ and have a Church to call Home.

What was it in me that assumed that joining a new church would resolve all of my woes and internal confusion?

It was residue from a Religious and Co-Dependent mindset. I wasn't just looking to visit and fellowship, I was looking to find somewhere to join so that my Acceptance tank could be filled. But God was calling me to first and foremost connect to corporate fellowship to gain strength and continue to build a solid, personal relationship with Him.

I needed to grow in discernment, intimacy, knowledge of the Word, taming my tongue and thoughts and most of all learn how to be guided and make decisions under His guidance and not from fleshly desire, ambition, or an unhealthy desire to please others. *Ouuuch*!! What a lesson! It's one that I have to keep at the forefront of my mind to avoid repeating it.

For three months, we successfully visited churches but there was an internal struggle within me that felt out of place and unsettled. *Was that a sign of Co-Dependency withdrawal and/or Anxiety?*

Philippians 4:6-8 says that we should:

> *"Be Anxious for nothing, but in everything by prayer and supplication with thanksgiving, let your requests be made known to God. And the peace of God, which surpasses all understanding, will guard your hearts and minds through Christ Jesus."* Amen.

Living from a place of anxiousness had become a way of life for me instead of the me being led solely by the Word of God. I needed to get back to the basics and reside there.

Sometimes our Internal navigation system needs to be realigned or jump-started to approach a matter from a different perspective.

Transition has always been an uncomfortable place for me. I could never fully accept the fact that the place of transition resembled how an airplane at times has a layover in one place before it heads to its' ultimate destination – it's a temporary stop, not a permanent place to set up shop.

There will be many of these along this Journey called Life so it would benefit us to get comfortable with being still

> **SIDE NOTE:** A great way to check in to see if we are making decisions from God's perspective vs external influence is to come to identify whether fear (*the root of anxiety and a whole bunch of other strongholds*) is present within us. When fear is present, it's best to Be Still and wait before proceeding forward.

and learn to be patient in places that are uncomfortable to our flesh and emotions. Speaking of taming emotions – well, that's another topic that I'll have to share with you about in another chapter or maybe even a book.

Let's get back to the story at hand…

In January, 2017, I was asked to minister the Word of God at a small local ministry for their morning service. That had been my second Ministry speaking assignment since I had left the previous church. Initially, I was reluctant because I didn't feel capable or qualified to minister to a congregation no matter how small it was.

> **SIDE NOTE:** Never rely on your feelings, they aren't always accurate. In fact, most of the time, they cannot be trusted.

After praying, I felt a sense of Peace. You see, I had a sincere desire to be used by God so this request seemed as if this opportunity was God orchestrated. I accepted and felt like a fish out of water trying to catch my breath throughout the entire sermon but I prayed that God was pleased and most of all Glorified.

I've always been timid when it came to speaking or doing anything that

I felt I hadn't "mastered" or completed training for; however, God had prepared me for that moment through all the practice sermons that my former Pastor had required us to facilitate as M.I.T.'s (Ministers in Training).

A few of the church members came up to me after the service and shared that they had been Blessed by the message, but I still felt that I lacked the qualification to stand behind God's Sacred desk.

It's not something that I take for granted or ever want to do from a fleshly mindset or perspective. At this moment, God reminded me that *"He doesn't call the qualified, He qualifies the called."* In short, what I saw as reluctance or fear was actually the tool God put in place to keep me humble and speak only what He wanted to be shared.

The Word of God says that:

"All scripture is God-breathed and is useful for teaching, rebuking, correcting and training in righteousness, so that the servant of God may be thoroughly equipped for every good work." – 2 Timothy 3:16-17

Anytime that I have been requested to share a message with God's people, I have been the first partaker and this time was no different.

My memory hasn't always cooperated to allow me to remember all of what God used me to share, but I clearly remember the theme of this particular message. A.I.M. – *Abide in Me!* It was a message from Jesus himself reminding us that we are supposed to *Abide in Him* at all times. The word Abide means: *to remain stable or fixed in a state* according to Merriam Webster dictionary.

As noted in John 14:4:

"Abide in Me, and I in you. As the branch cannot bear fruit by itself, unless it abides in the vine, neither can you, unless you abide in me."

That word brought me to a place of awareness about all that I had been experiencing the months and year leading up to that moment. It was a teaching, a rebuke, a correcting and a training on how to truly be still and know for myself that He **IS** God and recognize that apart from Him, I can do nothing!

On that same day, I was approached by the Senior Pastor with a proposition for her to cover me Spiritually as I would move forward into accepting future invitations to Minister and/or share empowerment through the books I've written.

Immediately, I not only felt that I had received an answer to my heartfelt prayers, but I also had this overwhelming sense of acceptance. Remember, I desired connection and acceptance. So, would I take the time to A.I.M. (Abide in Him) or would a familiar pattern arise once again? Would I be so infatuated by the need for acceptance and inclusion or would I go to a place of prayer to see what God's will was for the situation?

The initial verbal response that day was **YES**! This is an answer to my prayers but the internal thought was: *Slow down Dee!!! - Maybe you should pray about this!*

Once again, following God's Will for our lives cannot be based on our feelings, it must always be rooted and grounded in divine order according to the word of God, and a result of selfless prayer. This requires praying that the Will of God prevails and not what we desire to come to pass.

I accepted the offer from the Pastor to cover me and within weeks of beginning to visit, I also joined the ministry. I was immediately assigned to a Leadership role and served in the Church. Having a desire to help and to serve, but also having a tendency to move a little too fast, I found myself connected again, but *was this God's Divine Will?*

Both of the connections shared are related to Church; however, they can also be associated with any other role, position, or decision associated with Life. You see, we live in a microwave society desiring everything quickly, but that doesn't mean that we should make one or three- minute decisions. Decisions made quickly without prayer and wise counsel can prove costly.

Proverbs 11:14 says that:

"Where there is no counsel, the people fall; but in the multitude of counselors there is safety."

...not counselors from social media posts, but those we are led to through Holy Spirit.

Once again, I became a busy woman with my son in toe. Sure, the schedule was less religious or rigorous than before but I was still just going through the motions. I was "Doing Church" instead of being the Church.

During that year, I was ordained as a Minister of the Gospel in May 2017. This is an elevation that would have occurred within a few additional months at the former church had I not left abruptly. At that time, it seemed as though I would succumb to the stress (*literally*) had I not made the decision I had avoided for at least six months.

In January 2018, I made the decision that enough was enough already and resigned from my position and also left that ministry as well and as a result, the certificate of ordination was retracted. It seems that the more I invested in my relationship with God, the more I realized that serving in ministry at least in that capacity wasn't a mirror of my sweet spot. Not only that, but there was more Internal and Spiritual work that I had to undergo.

I guess by now you're thinking that this lady is unstable and has no idea what she wants out of life. If I was on the outside looking in, I would probably have the same thought.

The reality is that these two situations were just what was needed for me to get to a place of focus and soul searching to identify what was clouding my judgment and hindering my soul (mind, will and emotions) from being free and clear to make wise decisions, instead of taking on temporary connections that would make me feel good for a fleshly reason or temporary season.

What's the purpose of me sharing all of this? Trust me, there is a lesson in all of our experiences especially the ones where we are in the driver's seat. Let's explore some of my lessons here:

- Sometimes God allows conflict or confusion to grow us up and teach us how to Love Unconditionally and stand in the midst of adversity. Then there are other times when He sees that we need an extra push to move onto the next task or assignment that is purposed for our lives or the layer of healing/residue that He's trying to chisel off. I heard a saying recently that emphasizes this. "You can't heal in the same place where you got sick!" That environment or mindset for me was my Ambition.
- Our Mindsets and Behaviors are rooted in the experiences of our past and also the way we were raised. If we only acknowledge the patterns, but fail to do the work within to identify whether they are valid, healthy or just a means of survival for those who passed them down from generations then we are bound to repeat them.

- If the root of a behavior is never uprooted and inspected, we can never get to a place of real, raw, and permanent healing. Sometimes, you'll have to rip the band aid off, apply the antiseptic by way of facing the truth, and allow sufficient time for the wound to heal uncovered. In other words - **AIR IT OUT!** This requires vulnerability, transparency and the understanding that our processes will not be the same as that of someone else.

All of this revelation came during a time when I had been led to devote time to self-examination and self-care. A time to unearth the root of my issues. Listen – Never ask God to show you, *You* or what's hindering you if you really don't want to know the truth.

John 8:32 says:

> *"And you will know the truth and the truth will set you free."*

Facing your truth and seeking healing at all costs without shame is required to be set free to fully walk in Abundance, Success and live from a place of Victory.

Our Heavenly Father has already accepted us fully – flaws and all. Problems arise when we don't accept ourselves, fully understand the magnitude of His Love and neglect to place them in His hands. The moment we come to embody this truth is the turning point where we will be placed on the Potter's wheel again to experience another level of process, growth and transformation.

The process is that space in our lives that can be uncomfortable and we would love to run from or skip over, but because God Loves us so much, He doesn't allow us to.

It's a place where God stretches and fine tunes us into the image of His son Jesus Christ. It's a tight place, but a necessary one. It pushes us to the *throne of Grace, that we may obtain Mercy and find Grace to help in the time of need. – Hebrews 4:16*

In conclusion, the greatest lesson that I learned in this particular season of my life is that when we skip the process of excavation (clearing the land, healing, self-care, soul searching, etc.) it hinders us from building the new things in our lives on a clear and firm foundation.

I had to come to a place of acknowledging and commanding that every root of Fear, Rejection, unhealthy Acceptance from external connections, an estranged Mother/Daughter relationship, residue from broken relationships, Post-traumatic stress, etc., must be uprooted in order for the New Thing that God desired to build in and through my **Yes** to Him needed to be solid and free of contamination.

In addition, our decisions and connections must always be God-led, Inspired and Divinely Aligned. Time is up! There is no more time for decisions that are just good. Going forward, they must be God-Decisions. Otherwise, unfruitful cycles will be repeated.

If you're unclear of the Next step to take, I urge you to Abide and Seek God, He has ALL of the answers!

I'm so grateful that God extended His Grace to me when I was in denial about the fact that my land was full of debris. Today, I have surrendered and God is rebuilding every area of my Life on Cleared Land and I'm excited about what's to come. Stay tuned for my NEXT Chapter!

Debrayta (Dee) Salley *aka Dee Life Mentor Coach,* Founder of *Debrayta Salley Enterprises, LLC* is a Mother, Servant, Christian Author, Inspirational Speaker, Biblical Life Coach, Event Host and Wellness Advocate.

Her Life's Mission is to Empower Paths, Support Growth, and Inspire Change. She Supports/Serves Women of all ages through all phases of Life Transition and breaking free from any place, space or relationship where they may have settled for less than God's best.

CONNECT WITH ME:

WEBSITE: www.deelifmentor.com

SOCIAL MEDIA: @DeeLifMntrCoach
(FACEBOOK, INSTAGRAM, TWITTER)

I HAD TO DIE TO MYSELF SO I COULD LIVE AGAIN
A Time to be Born (Again) and a Time to Die (To Myself)
Author: Lena Dennis
Ecclesiastes 3:2a

It's amazing that after 65 years of living on this earth, I am still going through stuff. I realize that I will be tested and go through trials and tribulations until the day that I transition to my mansion in the sky.

One big difference within my current challenges is that I know better now who I am and whose I am. Back in the day, however, at the age of five, I remember not feeling like I was loved. True agape love conquerors all things but when there is an emptiness or void in you and you recognize it at an early age, *what do you do? And who do you tell about it?* This is especially hard when you don't know how to articulate your feelings.

Growing up in the 1950's-1970's, there was more freedom and less of a threat in letting your children roam the streets or go out and play in the neighborhood. Everyone knew each other and your "village" was in place. I was about 14 when that became real to me.

I was by the back gate of our home and I kissed a boy. Oh boy, was that the wrong thing to do!

My neighbor yelled out of their back door and by the time I entered the house, our phone was ringing. My Mom announced I was punished and I was put on notice about what would happen once she arrived home; she always kept her word too, so you can rest assured that I NEVER did that again! At least, not like that!

I was so used to being sneaky, lying, and being deceitful that I was very surprised that someone really noticed me rather positively or negatively. I craved attention not realizing that attention is not always a good thing. I was a young lady who was voiceless, lacked identity, suffered with low self-esteem, and was going through the motions.

As a young child, I would steal money from my Dad's money jar, run to the corner store, then sit in the hallway of the apartment building and eat myself silly with candy and all kinds of junk food! For a long time, I never got caught in the act, but my Dad must have had an idea because he started marking the jar. As a result, a few times I got spanked and punished and this was my wakeup call to learn that there is always a price to pay for a few moments of satisfying pleasure. I carried that mentality as I became a teenager and into adulthood.

My parents did the best they knew how to be. My issues were not only a part of the "Middle Child Syndrome," but it also stemmed from my feeling of inadequacy.

My oldest sister was "The Princess" and my youngest sister "The Spoiled Brat." I was told just recently that my parents believed that I didn't require a lot of attention because I did very well in school and was very self-sufficient and independent. This says a lot about perception and how other people see and label you based on an outside appearance.

You see, although I may have appeared this way on the outside, I was actually crying out from the inside in different ways. I had so many holes in my soul and didn't know how to fill them.

I was unknowingly open prey for the enemy who specializes in roaming to and fro looking for whom he can devour. Subsequently, I allowed myself to be used by many sexual liaisons which led to two pregnancies and two abortions by the age of eighteen. I had been taught that sex leads to pregnancy but never educated about using protection and what was available to prevent it. Naïve and vulnerable at an early age; I unfortunately learned the hard way what not to do.

When I was twenty-years-old, I met and married a young man that was charming and charismatic. I thought that I had arrived. The first day of our marriage, he left me and went to see his other woman. When I asked him about it, he beat me really badly.

Afterwards, his mom told me "Don't worry, you'll get used to it." For a whole year, I allowed myself to go through physical abuse. After having to seek medical attention a number of times because of the abuse, a doctor finally said to me "You will not be able to take this too much longer." I heard him loud and clear!

Although I returned to my abusive husband, the next time he came for me, I was washing dishes, and immediately grabbed the biggest knife I could find and commenced to swinging and cutting. That was the last day that we cohabited as a married couple. I came to the realization that he was a heroin addict. Although, I already knew that he indulged in marijuana, I didn't have much knowledge about any other drugs.

After this horrific part of my life, I was still looking for somebody or something to ease my pains, sorrows and hurts. Well, I was introduced to free-basing; also known as cocaine. Yes!! What a great way to lose yourself and escape from reality. It was my attempt to fill the holes that were in my soul!

I started using it every now and again, then progressing to being recreational. Eventually it led to a full-blown habit, and finally, an addiction. I was using it every day and all of the time. My thoughts were consumed with getting that next hit. It impacted all of my being and also my job.

Sleeping didn't matter, eating didn't matter, how I looked didn't even matter. All that mattered was the feeling of being on Cloud 9 from my drug of choice. It was never enough. I was always seeking to go higher and higher.

Ultimately, I eventually realized that cocaine couldn't take me to the heights that I wanted to experience. That's when I was introduced to the drug, heroin. Woo! Here I was, a sheep, headed for the slaughter!

I was really in the process of spiraling downward. Even though I had now become a functioning addict, my situation was destined to get worst. No good thing is achieved or gained while in the cycle of addiction or bad habits.

I was working for the Federal Government as a manager when I was around 35 years of age, I was single, and a hotmess.com. During this time, which was about the late 1980's, you were allowed to smoke in designated areas and the ladies room was one of them. I remember one day in particular, I clocked into work then retreated to the ladies' room, parked myself in the last stall and accompanied with my pipe, plenty of crack and lighters, smoked the entire shift without interruption! But God!!!!

Many times, I would send my clerks on drug runs for me. And yet, there is no documented evidence of drugs on any of my work records. As a matter of fact, when I left after 25 years of service, they could not locate any of my work records. Only God could promote you while you are out for suspension due to AWOL charges.

I was too busy getting high to answer the phone during my times of absence. The only explanation I can give is "Favor Ain't Fair" and BUT GOD!

It's not that I wasn't a great employee on my good days but that was becoming rare. The drugs took over my life and I was terminated for false allegations because of a personal vendetta from an upper manager. I wrote a letter rebutting the suspension and without representation. Within two weeks, I was back to work. I knew it was only a matter of time before there would be another issue so, I decided to work for one more year and then I resigned.

I lied to everyone by telling them that I was leaving to start my sewing business, but my inner truth and reality was that I was taking steps to become a full-time addict!

By this time, I had gotten married again, but this time to a great guy who was telling me about the God he served. He was oblivious to my addiction and became a great example of the fact that "Love covers a multitude of sins." Unconditional love was available even when I was unable to love myself. I stole from him several times and to this day, he has never confronted me about it.

During my struggle with drugs, I would even leave my husband because I realized the devastation that my lifestyle was infringing on his peace and well-being. I became a vagabond. I lived in abandoned houses, rented rooms, in drug houses, and visited soup kitchens regularly. Finally, after coming to the end of myself and taking off the many band aids, I returned to my marriage and a much better life. I wanted to quit abusing drugs too many times to count, but one day, I heard in something different in my spirit: *"No, this time you will go through to the end and I'll be waiting for you. You will be fine, but you must go to the end of this to never return."*

At first, I thought that I was receiving permission to do drugs! Now, I know that it was the beginning of me dying to self and living for God!

It's now been 14 years of no hard drugs! No heroin, no cocaine, no methadone, no rehab, no drug programs, no looking back. Only God can do that!

He cleaned me up and saved my life for His Glory. My God blessed me and I have had a prosperous sewing business for the last 15 years.

I serve as an Elder at the best church ever and I have to give Him all the Praise and Glory for transforming me and resurrecting my life! I was a sheep, headed for the slaughter, but God turned my life around and called me to be a shepherd to His sheep. Talk about a turnaround!!!

**I Had to Die to Myself so I could LIVE AGAIN
as a New Creation in Christ!**

Lena Maria Dennis is 65 years young and is living her Best Life! She has been married to Bruce Owen Dennis, Jr. for 24 years.

Her passion is her God-given talent as a Seamstress. For the last 15 years she has been the successful Business Owner and CEO of *Sew-So-Sassy, Inc.*

Prior to this, she worked at the Social Security Administration for 25 years. Along her journey, she has struggled with many life challenges. If it had not been for the Grace and Mercy of God, she knows that she would not have been able to endure them.

Lena cherishes each day as a gift and knows that her latter days are already and will continue to be better than her former days.

CONNECT WITH ME:
EMAIL: lenadennis5@gmail.com
FACEBOOK: @dressesbylena

NO LONGER BROKEN
A transparent and inspirational look at the life of a Godly Mother, Gigi, Counselor, Educator and Mentor
Author: Denise Madden
Ecclesiastes 3:3

The 3rd chapter of Ecclesiastes refers to seasons. Seasons are divisions of the year. In school, we were taught that there are four seasons: Winter, Spring, Summer, and Fall. As Christians, we go through stages of our lives that we can refer to as seasons. Just like seasons come and seasons go, so it is with the stages that we must go through.

I am going to discuss two of the seasons mentioned in Ecclesiastes 3; *a time to break down, and a time to build up*. I am a testimony of how God broke down and built things up in your life.

When things are breaking down, it means they are falling apart, collapsing, or shattering. There are many situations in our lives like divorce, death, loss of a job, child moving out, that can be considered as breakdowns. When thinking of breakdowns, try not to get discouraged, because, God can build you back up.

When breaking down involves going through a divorce, it is imperative that one must lean on the Spirit of God for healing. Healing will not occur overnight. and going through a divorce or any situation deemed difficult can be a challenging process.

In some cases, it requires us to pray for forgiveness and deliverance. When breakdowns occur, it is helpful to not only seek God, but also to read books, and spend time with Him. It is best not to isolate yourself, because it is during those times that the enemy will come in and try to wreak havoc in your mind.

When going through a divorce, I spent many days and nights in my room crying uncontrollably. I did not want to get out of bed, and I did not think I would ever get better. The enemy tried to convince me to commit suicide; however, I knew that would cause me to go to hell, which was not an option. Finally, I woke up one day and thought, this is enough.

I have three amazing kids, and a rambunctious grandson who need me. My oldest daughter would plan things for my kids and I to do, so that I could get out of the house. This helped me to live one day at a time, and one day, I finally felt free. God had delivered me from depression and brought me through by the Grace of God. Hallelujah!

Years later, my oldest daughter decided to move into her own place with my grandson. Although, I was proud of her for making an independent decision, I was devastated. You see, this Momma Bear likes to keep her cubs close. It was difficult, but God saw me through it.

God led me to enroll into school and I earned a Master of Education in School Counseling from Liberty University in Lynchburg, Virginia. My graduation day was so exciting. Not only because my daughter's graduation was the next day, but because it was a journey that was ending. My Mom, oldest daughter, and grandson got up early in the morning to travel to Lynchburg.

Before getting on the road, we stopped to fill the tire because it seemed to be losing air. As we traveled about three hours, we heard a loud noise. As it turned out, the tire blew, and I had to pull over on the side of the road. Even though I contacted emergency assistance, someone from the Department of Transportation arrived seconds later to assist. They put the spare tire on, and we were on our way.

Upon arriving at my graduation, it appeared chaotic. I had to quickly determine where to go; however, I did arrive before the processional. The ceremony was amazing, the Vice President of the United States spoke, the praise and worship team sang under the anointing, and it was turning out to be a great day, so far.

After the ceremony, I was to proceed to another location for my degree presentation. Due to the amount of traffic and being told by two different people who provided two different places where I had to go, I missed my degree presentation. As you can imagine, I was heartbroken, disappointed, and completely devastated; however, I had to get over it, because we had to get back on the road to attend my daughter's ceremony in Hampton. My family and I had a great time in Hampton, not only celebrating her graduation but celebrating Mother's Day as well.

Graduation was over, which meant it was time to work. Because the summer was upon us, I was unable to work for my school system. So, I began sending out resumes.

I went on four interviews and received job offers from *all* of them. We serve a mighty God!

I sought God, who led me to the position I was supposed to accept. It was extremely exciting to be earning a paycheck again. Prior to that, I was on educational leave without pay and completing two internships, which lasted almost a year. You may ask how I survived without a consistent paycheck; all I can say is that *God provides*. Money came from unexpected sources.

As we progress through this journey called life, God will sometimes break us down to build us up. We don't always understand what God is doing. We don't always see the big picture; however, God wants us to put our trust in Him.

After going through everything, and I didn't even share it all, God spoke to me and said, "*Restoration*." Just that word alone brought hope, comfort, excitement, and peace.

You see my friend, when God speaks a word to your heart, you can count on it being done. When He spoke it, I was excited, because I know what it means for God to restore everything that was lost.

My expectations are that God is going to send a suitable mate for me, provide a new place for me to live, and build up everything that has been broken down.

As I write this, the only thing I can do is say that *God is Real, He is Faithful, He is a Provider, and He Loves His children.* When you are faced with situations that you don't understand, seek God. Our lives are in His control when we give it to Him. What this means is that, He orchestrates our steps in His own timing.

At times we may pray, and it may seem like our prayers are hitting a brick wall; however, that may be God's way of telling us that the time is not right. Also, the Word of God tells us that sometimes He answers immediately; however, the prince and power of the air can try to cause a delay, which God may allow.

God knows that if He gives us things that we are not ready for, it may bring heartache, apply financial strain and cause confusion; and we know that God is not the author of confusion. God sees the *big* picture. We may only see parts, but God sees the whole.

Sometimes, it's difficult to trust in a God that we cannot see or physically touch, but we can hear His still small voice, and we can feel Him. We can experience Him as He turns situations around in our lives. Especially situations that only He could have changed. God loves us so much, and He knows what is best for us. So, don't be discouraged if you lose a house, that means He has a better one for you. Don't be disappointed if you lose a job, that means He has a better one for you. Don't worry if the guy or lady you were seeing is no longer interested, that means God has someone better. I assure you that God breaks down to build up.

Sometimes it's difficult for us to trust the process. It is the process that helps us grow. It is the process that teaches us to trust God. It is the process that shows us that God loves us, and that He is in control. It is the process that teaches us patience. Until we get to the point of trust, God will continue to bring situations in our lives to cause us to trust Him.

I'm talking about the situations that you don't see your way out of. Situations that man cannot bring you out of. Situations where only a miracle can alter it.

Proverbs 3:5 says,

    "Trust in the Lord with all thine heart, and lean not unto thine own understanding, in all thy ways acknowledge Him, and he shall direct thy path."

This means we must trust God, and not our infinite minds. In everything that we do, we should acknowledge Him, and He shall direct our paths. You see, when we step out of the way, and allow God to direct our paths, then we are safe, we are protected, and we are covered. However, if we try to do things on our own, without God's wisdom or without God's direction, we can mess things up badly.

But because of God's grace, and the fact that He loves us so much, He will still help us through when trials come our way. In other words, before we get to "Z," we have to start with "A." While we are going through, we should praise Him, we should study His word, and we should seek Him. This will provide strength for us to endure. We should also seek wise counsel, when necessary. It is not catastrophic to seek counsel; but rather it is wise. As Christians, we have an advantage; we have help and we are not alone. The help I am referring to is the calm, gentle, and sweet Holy Spirit, who gives us access to the Father.

Ephesians 2:18 says,

> *"For through him, talking about the Holy Spirit, we have access by one spirit unto the Father."*

Did you notice that the word of God refers to the Holy Spirit as Him? The Holy Spirit is the 3rd person of the trinity, which means He is a "Him," and not an "it." As Christians, it is so important to have a firm foundation. The foundation is prayer and knowledge of the Word of God.

I accepted Jesus Christ as my Lord and Savior on March 6, 1983 and was filled with the Baptism of the Holy Spirit the following Sunday, which was Pentecost Sunday. As a teenager, my Mom would not only take me to church and bible study, but she also took me to prayer meetings each week, which took place in people's homes.

Because of the firm foundation, I have learned to pray and allow the Holy Spirit to lead and guide me. Do I make mistakes? Of course, I do. Have I stumbled along the way? You bet I have; however, I was smart enough to know that I can go back to my kind and loving God to pick me up. We will make mistakes, because we are human and imperfect. However, we must go to God and ask for forgiveness and true repentance.

My friend, please understand that this Christian walk is not always a happy place. There are trials and tribulations, that we must go through to make us stronger. But I can assure you that you won't go through things alone.

On one side you have goodness, and on the other side you have mercy – not to mention the Father, the Son, and the Holy Spirit. We are not set up to fail, but rather, we are set up to win. The end of the book of Revelation lets us know that we win!

God wants us to be successful. He loves us and wants the very best for us. However, we must be obedient to Him and to His word. To be able to be obedient to Him, and to His word, we must read it. Life can get so busy with serving in the Church, taking care of children, working, taking care of a spouse or loved ones; however; we must take time to read God's word and establish and maintain a prayer life; especially if we are seeking Him for His will in our lives. His will for us can be revealed in His word. His word is a road map for us, it provides instructions, answers to prayers, and guidance.

So, you see my friend, God provides us with the tools we need to be successful; however, it is up to us to use them. God is a gentleman, and He gives us free will. So, He is not going to force us to follow His path, but He will gently direct us. This is what I love about God.

Philippians 4:19 says,

> *But my God shall supply all your need according to His riches in glory by Christ Jesus."*

This means God gives us what we need. When we lack something, we can go to Him, because He is our source. Who wouldn't want to serve a God like that?

Not only does He provide for our needs, but He loves us unconditionally. This means regardless of what we do, God still loves us. We must be so careful how we treat Him. He is a jealous God, and He does not want us to place anyone before Him. He wants to be our focus. He knows we must work, and attend to the cares of life; however, He also wants us to acknowledge and make time for Him.

Hopefully, you understand there are times to break down, and times to build up. If a building or situation isn't broken down, then how can it be built up? It is the breaking down that God uses to build character in us. Not only that, but we realize our strength, and our dependence on God. Praise the Lord!

So, I encourage you to go through your broken-down state with grace, with humility, and with trust that God will build everything back up again. This is the Word of God, and His word is true.

As God provided the words for this chapter, my prayer was and still is, that God would help you during your difficult times, struggles, and the times when you don't understand what is going on in your life. During those times, put your complete trust in God.

May God richly bless and keep you and your family until He comes again. Remember, there is a season that includes a time to break down, and a time to build up. Walk gracefully through whatever season that God has for you currently. God bless you!

Denise L. Madden is a mother of three amazing children: London, age 26, Maci, age 22, and Jadon, age 16. She is also a proud Gigi to Collin, age 7.

She has earned a Master of Education in School Counseling from Liberty University, a Bachelor of Science in Interdisciplinary Studies from Stevenson University, an Associate of Arts in Elementary Education from Community College of Baltimore County, and an Associate of Arts in Legal Secretarial Studies, with a Minor in Word Processing from Villa Julie College.

Denise is an Educator, Counselor, and Mentor. She enjoys serving in her church, traveling, and spending time with her children. She has been blessed with the life-changing opportunity to serve in Guatemala and Haiti.

Denise is excited about her writing career. Her passion and prayer are to impact and encourage, while letting readers know that they can always trust God to see them through life's obstacles.

CONNECT WITH ME:
EMAIL: denisemadden1021@gmail.com
PHONE NUMBER: (410) 982-3154

A PLAN BEHIND THE PAIN
Author: Mitzi L. Carrasquillo

A time to weep, and a time to laugh;
a time to mourn, and a time to dance;
Ecclesiastes 3:4a-b

"HELL NO, I WANT TO LIVE!!"

Those words still sit with me today...

It was in that moment at Boston Medical Center that I knew my mom was serious about life. It was December 18, 2016, our third emergency room visit in one month. As she laid there with her oxygen mask, she removed it and said *"ask him Mitzi."* I smiled and said OK. She put her oxygen mask back on and waited as Dr. Doug came back in the room. As he's tending to her, she gives me the "look."

I said: *"Excuse me Dr. Doug, do you think, eventually, she can get a mobile oxygen tank"*? Dr. Doug said, *"Um, we can discuss that at a later date, right now we want her to get better."* He then added, *"please do not ever drive her here again that was very dangerous, call 911, they have oxygen in the ambulance that you don't have in your car."* My husband Jose and I looked at each other and nodded (rolling our eyes), smiling, knowing all the red lights he ran.

When Dr. Doug stepped out the room again, we had a good laugh. Ma took her mask off and said *"what did he say about the machine?"* I told her he said we can discuss at a later date. Ma sucked her teeth and in her only Jean can say voice, *"I'll be dead by then!"* While still looking at her I said, *"Ma, don't say that."*

It was at that time I noticed a sadness came over her face that moved me. To lighten up this dreary emergency room, I tried to make a joke out of it, I said to ma "*Aren't you gonna be embarrassed walking around with the oxygen tank?*" She looked me straight in the face and said "HELL NO I WANT TO LIVE!!" She said, "*Plus, they got cute ones now, like a pocketbook!*" All of us burst out laughing!!

Eighteen days later on Tuesday, January 3, 2017, my heart was completely broken. My mom, my love and best friend was gone.

And I will pray the Father, and he shall give you another Comforter, that he may abide with you forever; John 14:16

Driving to her house, I knew something was wrong. I felt it in my spirit., I was uneasy, worried and found myself extremely anxious. I had left numerous voice messages and texts to her. My heart was racing, my arms and legs were shaking as my husband tried to ensure me everything would be OK. A Smokey Robinson song came on the radio, my husband said see, she's OK, there's Smokey. We smiled. She was his biggest fan. But I knew something was wrong, she had a bad habit of not answering her phone, but this was different. None of her kids had heard from her all day today; very unusual.

I heard the screams as we entered the elevator on the first floor. She lived on the 4th floor so, I called 911 as soon as we entered the elevator, praying that we didn't lose connection. As the doors opened, there was my baby brother, Damien (and his girlfriend trying to compose him) storming the 4th floor hallway, screaming "My mom is dead!" Still on the phone with 911, my husband and I took off running down the hall, through the crowd of her neighbors, onlookers and EMTs. I started yelling to the police "I'm her daughter," as I pushed through the crowd that formed.

I fell to my knees the moment I laid eyes on her. I knew she was gone.

There she was, still in bed with her beautiful pink flowered pajamas, with her glasses on and her cell phone still at her ear. Her hands were clutched to her chest with her mouth open, head tilted back as if she cried out in such pain. I was literally in shock and agony. Hysterically crying, I tried to move her, thinking she will wake up. The stiffness and coldness of her body made me realize she was not sleeping and I was not dreaming, hallucinating or going crazy.

I moved about focusing and reviewing everything in the room, trying to somehow make some sort of sense. The television was on, roll of toilet tissue on the left at the top of the bed, the throat lozenges my son gave her on the top right of the bed and her nebulizer to left at her head.

As we began to pray and lay hands on her, I noticed her phone charger cord sticking out from under her back. I lifted her a bit to remove it as if it was hurting her. Once my husband and I finished praying, I made two calls prior to calling my siblings. I called my sister in law, Diana and my girlfriends, Carol and Jeannette. All of them are prayer warriors that God lead me contact to set the atmosphere for spiritual support during this time of pain, sorrow and total chaos.

We began to make the calls to all of my siblings, my mom's siblings and her best friend Christine. While still answering the police and EMT's questions of her health issues, last time anyone physically seen her and spoke to her, trying to put together some sort of a timeline etc. we noticed her dog, Ginger barked for an extremely long time and was so traumatized of everything and all the people. We know she knew and sensed what had happened.

During Ma's 73 years, she suffered from Chronic Obstructive Pulmonary

Disease (COPD) and had three previous heart attacks, we can only assume this was another and took her precious, loving life.

The medical examiner informed us that there would be no autopsy, since mom's death was not considered a homicide. After the state photographer arrived, took his pictures of her still in the bed and the EMT took his information relaying it to the medical examiner via phone, he asked did I have a funeral home to come get mom. Never experienced this, I said Lord what do I do? My heart was so broken and I was so baffled, it was only the grace of God that kept me.

Seeing her all alone, all I could do is cry, kiss and tell her how sorry I was as the funeral home came to retrieve her body. I begin to remove her anklets and jewelry that she loved so much. As my brother Lorenzo and other siblings arrived, the pain of watching our mother of seven, grandmother of seven and great grandmother of two be placed in a bag, the sound of the zipper, the unforgettable sound of the clunk of her beautiful body being placed on the stretcher and wheeled out of the apartment, down the hall was beyond heart-wrenching. It felt like I was watching a movie, like I was in an out-of-body experience. All I kept thinking was that this was not real. It seemed as if we had just laughed about my husband's birthday, his age, said our love you's and chuckled at saying *"See you next year."*

> *Beauty for ashes and provide for those who grieve in Zion—*
> *to bestow on them a crown of beauty*
> *instead of ashes,*
> *the oil of joy*
> *instead of mourning,*
> *and a garment of praise*
> *instead of a spirit of despair.*
> *They will be called oaks of righteousness,*
> *a planting of the Lord*
> *for the display of his splendor. Isaiah 61:3*

As she called us, *Jean's "Lucky Seven,"* Mom was all we had, she was always there for everyone whether it was making potato salad, macaroni salad, coconut cake, crocheting beautiful blankets, scarfs, baby sweater sets, etc. She was a social butterfly, went to everyone's parties, cookouts, graduations, you name it, she was there. She had a full social life with her family, friends and crochet groups. She really was her senior citizen group in one :)

She always wanted a family photo of her four sons and three daughters together, but there was always one or two of us missing in the picture. She was so funny; she would take those family photos and try and put them together in a frame or would even place them on the wall next to each other. We'd laugh at her living room wall of her homemade family photo, this was always her requested gift for Mother's Day, her birthday, Christmas, really ANY DAY… It had become the running joke in the family.

There we were all seven of us in her living room spread out on her floor and new couches (she would of have had a fit:)), putting disagreements aside, making our way through the details and planning of our mom's homegoing services.

Before we started planning, we began holding hands, as my sister Krystal led us in prayer, I know mom would have been so proud of us. We made and assumed tasks, making decisions on details of her life/obituary, pictures to use, food, music, scriptures, cleaning out her apartment, settling her personal issues, welcomed and met with out of state family and friends, etc.

My siblings and I were so busy and focused that we really couldn't even think about the grief process. The real work begins when you get home, having true confession and conversation with yourself.

> *"Blessed are they that mourn; for they shall be comforted." Matthew 5:4*

> *I have seen their ways, but I will heal them;*
> *I will guide them and restore comfort to Israel's mourners,*
> *creating praise on their lips. Isaiah 57:18*

Just when we thought we were somewhat catching our breathe and acknowledging this weakness to get to our breakthrough, our baby brother, Damien was murdered.

My husband and I was awoken out of our sleep when we received a call at 11:45 pm. He had been shot and we were to come to Boston Medical Center, as soon as possible. No other details were provided other than to hurry up. As my husband and I threw on some clothes, rushed to the car, drove out from our street two blocks and while sitting at the set of lights we received another call asking were we on the way? I said yes, they said "I just wanted to let you know you won't be able to see his body." I said huh? And "what do you mean *his body*?" It was in that moment we learned that Damien was gone. I yelled out a cry of misery, my husband and I sat at the light then pulled over and wailed.

He was killed in a drive by shooting on August 14, 2017. Our hearts were broken again…just seven months after mom.

I reflect often back to our last conversation and the last time I saw him at the family cookout two weeks prior. Him there, smiling, clowning, bragging about how he has "*mom's potato salad recipe down pat.*" I teased him that I need to sample it; we laughed and left off talking about the planning of a memorial gathering on mom's upcoming birthday on September 11th. I was telling him that it was too soon for me to have a big gathering, but maybe we can all get together for dinner, just us kids? He said sure and he'd bring the potato salad and did a dance and smirk to show off. My husband and I burst out laughing, gave him a hug as he walked us to the car said our love you's and we drove off. Even as we were driving off, he was doing an imitation of one of our family members as we're cracking up out the car window.

That was unfortunately our last time together. Damien was just 36 years old; so full of life and I'd have to say the most "family oriented" of all. He never missed a family gathering or event and was always thinking of an idea to try and get us together for something.

He never saw it coming. All we know is that it was instant and suddenly we are beyond devastated. He did not deserve to have his life taken as such, no one does. To date, his murder is unsolved. The pain, hurt and anger of losing him was simply devastating. I knew solved or unsolved, I must walk in complete forgiveness.

Forgiveness does not mean forgetting, nor does it mean disregarding or justifying offenses. It means that I will not drink the poison of hating someone or kill myself physically, mentally, emotionally and spiritually. Me hating the person(s) will do nothing but keep me in anger, bitterness and pain. Forgiving is a powerful part of the healing process: it clears the mind, body and spirit. It is not my job to seek revenge, that is not for me to do. I stay in prayer and trust in God, knowing that revenge is His.

"Vengeance is mine; I will repay, saith the Lord"--Romans 12:19;

"For vengeance I would do nothing. I will turn their mourning into gladness; I will give them comfort and joy. Jeremiah 31:13

Losing mom was as if life ended and would never be the same; she was all we had. With her and now my brother gone, I lost myself. There are times when I literally don't/didn't know who I was crying for, whether I was coming or going.

I couldn't sleep and would cry at night in bed with my face in the pillow (so my husband couldn't hear me) or in my car. In those quiet moments alone were the most painful, especially in the shower, to screaming at the top of my lungs (on my knees) when no one was there. The pain was indescribable!

Some days, I just didn't want to get out of bed. Not wanting to get out of bed or attend gatherings became a sign and turning point for me. I knew I could not move forward until the grief was addressed and I truly felt the pain.

After both of the services were over, many people would say, "Let me know if you need anything or if there is anything I can do." That always nice to hear, but in the end, you must do the work of self, through the grace of God.

Please do not go through this alone; the hurt controls your healing process. Bring your grief to God in prayer, He is a voice for the dead and the living. He will allow you to rest in His peace.

> Earth has no sorrow that Heaven cannot heal...
> 'He will wipe every tear from their eyes. There will be no more death'
> or mourning or crying or pain, for the old order of things has passed.
> Revelations 21:4

> Give all your worries and cares to God, for he cares about you. 1 Peter 5:7

The healing process has been just that, a process... Healing isn't pretty, grief is a significant life change and change of lifestyle. You cannot run away or silence the pain.

I can go from crying at the drop of a hat, whether it's a memory, driving by her senior citizen building, looking at a picture or hearing a Smokey Robinson song. I severely endured the hurt, pain, sadness, loneliness, emptiness, anger, because I was yearning for her voice, kiss, hugs, simply the complete essence of her. It was only when I began to understand my behavior changes and receive instruction that I gained a full understanding that God's Word never changes. He knew exactly what I was going through and how to address my pain.

But you are a chosen people, a royal priesthood, a holy nation, God's special possession, that you may declare the praises of him who called you out of darkness into his wonderful light. 1Peter 2:9

I had prerequisites from my Lord. He gave me the same words and tools that He provided me in my journey to overcome unaddressed childhood sexual abuse, teenage rape, depression and contemplating suicide.

Although He let me know that my life was not defined by abuse, the characteristics and darkness that I was once delivered from (pain, hurt, trauma, fear, guilt, shame, unloved, loneliness), then returned just in a different form.

Death of anything is painful, hurtful and traumatizing. The comparison to how I was feeling of the loss reminded me so much of the abuse I overcame. I began to walk in guilt for not being there with mom then, hurt and fear for what happened to Damien. I was feeling shame and a loss of love for no longer having them here. Unexpected death is lonely and exhausting. I simply found myself not having the right words to express how I felt; sometimes even not knowing what to say at all.

Jesus Christ is the same yesterday and today and forever. Hebrews 13:8

During this season of grief, mourning and restoration, my joy left me. I no longer wanted to be bothered with anyone or anything. There were times I couldn't speak of her without breaking down in tears, and I couldn't sleep without crying.

Seeing women mom's age and older enjoying life, dancing, listening to music and out with their friends sometimes brings me a sort of sadness.

God's presence and love for me was truly felt. He knew what I was going through and surrounded me such beautiful sisters in Christ; true prayer warriors and ministers of His Word. Many of them had also lost their mother and were able to really understand, be non-judgmental and sympathize with what I was going through while lovingly informing me of what to expect.

I've heard it said that God is responsible for your healing but you are responsible for your health. I had to be vulnerable and go inside to heal, I had to feel it.

Talking to family and others helps to keep her memory alive. In sharing stories and sowing into others helps me to heal while moving forward. I also took the opportunity to attend and participate in several healing conferences and workshops.

> *Beloved, I pray that all may go well with you and that you may be in good health, as it goes well with your soul. 3 John 2*

One of the main resources that we are provided (that many shy away from) is therapy. Talking to a licensed/mental health professional or just simply talking to someone you can trust definitely can help. To successfully overcome the stages of grief (denial, anger, depression and acceptance), you must share and release the emotions. Be honest and know that there is nothing wrong with crying. That is the journey to healing your wounds. God gave us these emotions to use; keeping everything inside is such an invisible wound. Take it one day at a time, don't be afraid to ask questions or seek assistance.
Moving forward has been such a faith walk. Faith truly does make things

possible, not easy. I learned to live with grief, celebrating them while keeping them in my heart forever.

In understanding this graceful season of weeping and mourning, I've realized life is simply precious. The Bible says we are here like a vapor, here and then, we are gone.

> *Why, you do not even know what will happen tomorrow. What is your life? You are a mist that appears for a little while and then vanishes. James 4:14*

Enjoy every little and big moment, laugh, dance and be encouraged. Have a vision of hope and restore your soul as tomorrow is not promised. The enemy comes to steal, kill and destroy not only our life, but literally the life out of us.

Weeping, laughing, mourning and dancing are all a part of our life experiences. The suffering will not last forever if you trust and allow the joy of the Lord to be your strength. Not all of my days are good, but I know I am more than a conqueror. God is loving, healing and restoring me and He gets the last word.

> *His divine power has given us everything we need for a godly life through our knowledge of him who called us by his own glory and goodness. 2 Peter 1:3*

"To encourage and empower others that there is recovery after every storm..."

Mitzi L. Carrasquillo is a Childhood Sexual Trauma Recovery Coach, Author and Speaker. Victoriously surviving sexual abuse and rape, Mitzi's primary purpose in life is to love, heal, and restore all women suffering from Childhood Sexual Abuse and Teenage Rape. She has great love and compassion for all people and has diligently served as a Victim Advocate.

There is nothing that we cannot overcome through the power of God. Many of us experience mental or emotional issues that stem from mental, physical, or emotional abuse that have left us with feelings of powerlessness, resentment and shame. Yet, the Greater One resides on the inside, and through it all, we are still overcomers. God's love, healing, and restoration changed her life and has given her the courage and strength to move forward in her assignment to help others.

Mitzi resides in Brockton, Massachusetts, married to her husband Jose, and has three children and four grandchildren.

CONNECT WITH ME:
PHONE: 301-536-3662
EMAIL: mitzi@LovedHealedandRestored.com
WEBSITE: www.LovedHealedandRestored.com
FACEBOOK:
www.facebook.com/LovedHealedandRestored

MY FATHER'S DAUGHTER
A Time to Love and a Time to Hate
Author: Mae Golden
Ecclesiastes 3:8

I HATED HIM! *Not to put too fine of a point on it!*

I'd like to say that one of my earliest memories of my dad was one of Joy with an image of me bouncing on his knee, being thrown up in the air and then being caught by him. Unfortunately, that's not my story.

My dad was a broken man: however, it was an undiagnosed brokenness. It was evident to most and un-intervened by all.

My first memory of him was him in a rage. He slammed a plate of spaghetti with tomato sauce against the wall, breaking the plate, then slapped my mother across our one-bedroom apartment, out of the front door, down the steps, into and through our downstairs neighbor's apartment, out of their back door and up the stairs back into our apartment. At the time, I was just 3 years old.

After this horrible encounter, my mom cleaned up the mess he had made, while he disappeared into their bedroom or somewhere out of the apartment. Witnessing this early on in life, convinced me that power was had by those who were bigger, louder and physically threw their weight around. It also gave me the impression and mindset that I had no power. I would spend my life yearning for it.

It is the experiences of our youth that form our belief systems, behaviors and reactions. As a result, I've spent my life fearing almost everything and everyone. I've also maintained an inner rage against my aggressors, both actual and perceived. You see, sometimes in life, we think that people are against us, but they really are not. Sometimes we are really against ourselves and don't know how to live differently.

As a child, I was always running home from school, crying, to keep from being beaten up by someone about something. I got to be really good at running. Quite fast, actually.

If I was met by my dad at the front door in tears, I lied and said I had a headache, stomach ache or something because if my dad saw me crying and knew the real reason, I would have to go back out and *"beat their a## or come back home to get my a## beat by him."* So, I quickly learned how to develop my own alternatives and defense mechanisms.

I hated fighting. I grew up in a home that had enough of that. Whenever he drank, he became belligerent and violent. Often my mother was threatened with a weapon and/or an actual beating with his fists. Plus, being the youngest, I had my share of being picked on by my siblings. That was short lived though, because we were a blended family and they were much older.
I didn't have the tenacity, or the high pain threshold required to take a punch and remain standing. Or worse yet, not cry. My spirit was tender and quiet, just like my mother's.

As an adult, I equated that tender and quiet spirit as weak or powerless. You know the type, the one who may try to get in one good lick before being pummeled by their aggressor. Being on the receiving end of that type of pummeling makes you think twice before trying to defend yourself again. Well, I gave my life to the Lord and that made everything better. Sike! (*just kidding*).

I received Jesus Christ as my Lord and Savior when I was 15 years old. Reclaimed, as it were. My first 'saving' time was when I was 12 years old. I was brought to the cross by my Christian mom and newly saved dad.

They said they didn't want to see me burn in hell. By the time they finished scaring me, I cried out for salvation, as I knew it. (I later understood I was actually crying out for fire insurance as I really didn't know anything about sin, being saved, or redeemed, except that it made my dad act kinder and sweeter to us and we went to church as a family. So, ok, I want in too – *smile*.)

A few months later though, he got angry about something one of the auxiliary groups he'd became a member of did and we stopped attending church. Again, to be quite honest, I still didn't know anything about sin or a life of it, so being 'saved' had no hold on me. I was 12 after all and rarely went outside or mingled with others. *What was I being 'redeemed' from exactly?*

Besides, I didn't like having to wear dresses all the time anyway. At the age of 15, at the urging of a classmate, I went back to church. The result was a commitment to Christ on my own. All I knew then was that I loved Him and wanted to live for Him.

In hindsight, I realize that often those who teach from the pulpit or the floor, teach based on their experience, understanding and possibly more importantly, what they have been taught. I thought that their word was 'Gospel' and didn't question it. I didn't read the Bible on my own with a 'reflective method' which prompted questions for more insight. I just took the Bible at what it said. Period – The End.

As I understood it, if you acted wrong God, your Heavenly Father, would strike you down. I mean, we all know that you reap what you sow. That was evidenced by the explanations given for why folk got sick, got into trouble, lost their stuff or their stuff broke. It was because God was punishing them for sinning.

So, now the new person in my life wielding the Power was God. I spent a good portion of my adult life seeing God as one on whose bad side I didn't want to be on. I appreciated Jesus, His Son, for all that He did for me on the cross. I was finally saved, though I could lose it at any time because of my sin. And I enjoyed His Holy Spirit, who seemed to touch me every Sunday and made me jump around and fall out. Then He later gave me a dance. (*I loved to dance, even as a child. Yeah! I had moves!*).

But my rage continued to build and reside on the inside of me. It took me years recognize it as rage though, because I was a Christian and we don't get angry, much less act out in rage. And after all, wasn't I satisfied with Jesus alone?!?

Fast forward to the year 2010, while at a ⁱJoyce Meyer Women's Conference, I realized that the rage was there, and it needed to be dealt with. The topic of one of the speakers dealt with fathers and their roles in protecting their daughters. I sat there and bawled my eyes out, because not once did I ever feel protected by my dad. I referred to him as my father when speaking to others, but the title to me belied the protector element.

- When I was in 2nd grade and brought home a 2nd place ribbon for the 100-yd dash from my school's Field Day, he was the one who wanted to know *"why didn't you get 1st place?"*
- When I was 10 years old, after requesting that I make and bring him an Alka Seltzer, he spit it out onto my back when I turned around to walk away. And no, he didn't say he that was sorry, nor did he acknowledge that he'd done it.
- When I was 12 or 13 years old, I was outside playing in the street with a group of kids and heard what I thought was someone screaming out in pain. It was coming from my house. I ran up to my front door and swung it open. He responded in a half question half statement taunting way, *"You thought I was beatin' yo' mama's a##!?"* So - Protector? No way.
- The speaker went on to relate that our Heavenly Father is always there for us. Yeah, ok. I accepted it but didn't really believe it. I also realized that my rage towards my Dad needed to be dealt with and cleaned out.

As I reflected on how I would be able to move forward and do this, I also began to realize another thing: Some characteristics I hated about my dad, I exhibited. Most notably, the need to be right and followed. "*Just do what I said*." Highly opinionated. Ugh!!!! I was a LOT like him. I look more like him than I do my Mom. I am also physically built like him. There is nothing worse as a woman than feeling you look manly. Eeeuuu! Sorry, I digress.

The conference helped me to see the tip of this proverbial rage iceberg and I started chipping away at it. My 'chip away' began in a Walmart parking lot, after I returned home from the conference. Here is where my thoughts came to a head. This was not my plan. It just happened; and let it.

I began to address my dad as if we were sitting on a Dr. Phil stage and I screamed, "*Why did you treat me like that? What did I ever do to you? Do you understand the trauma you caused? Do you know how much I have hated you? Why did you treat my mother like that?*" etc. etc. etc.

My tears rolled freely down my face as did the snot and I had to blow my nose several times in order to adequately breath. Yes, it was the <u>*ugly*</u> cry. I cried so hard that I had to pull over in the parking lot, taking up several spaces, as I was blocking traffic beforehand and had to get it all out before going home. But this was only the tip of the iceberg. I felt better. At least at that moment.

It would be much later when I tackled the larger portion of iceberg under the water line. Besides, I didn't have time to process much else right then. I had other things to do. Like getting my groceries home, cooking dinner, preparing for work the next day…. you know, stuff.

Four years later my life was falling apart at the seams. All the life-type stuff was going on: chronic illness had found a home at my house, my children were all adults and had moved to various parts of the globe (*translation: now what do I do?*); my marriage was not where I thought it should be; my job sucked; lastly, my relationship with God was on the low fire of lukewarm.

At the beginning 2015, during a Saturday morning praise and worship portion of a women's fellowship at my church, I started to weep uncontrollably. Now, that is normal for some and used to be normal for me, but I had since thrown that aside after my newfound understanding that I had really used worship to hide my hurts, disappointments and discouragements.

My tears could flow, and no one would ask what was wrong or *if* something was wrong. It was assumed that *this* was the way I worshiped. And I mean, it was the way I worshiped. It's just that when I gained this new understanding, I felt that I shouldn't use worship that way. Rather, I should do something different, but what, I didn't know.

So, during this time of worship, I was totally caught off guard by my tears and the lack of control on my part. Fortunately, I didn't fight this second Walmart moment but flowed with it. God spoke to my heart and said, "*That idol had to fall. Things had to happen the way they did, otherwise you would not grow.*"

The 'idol' He referred to was something that occurred about a year and a half earlier. That situation put my life into a tailspin and truly ROCKED my world in all the wrong ways. All stability emotionally and mentally was lost and a rage, THAT rage, boiled internally like hot lava. This time, I was FULLY aware of it and was actively trying to keep it under wraps. Unfortunately, this time I also had given it a reign that only a devote, holy ghost filled and fire baptized Saint could. It had housing, a car and full permission to every room in my heart, figuratively speaking.

The weight of my emotions and thoughts were such that I thought I would break. Those months took my strength, my peace and my fellowship with God. At this point in my spiritual walk, the one thing I knew was that I couldn't live without my fellowship, no matter how demoralized I felt. I knew that God still cared.

A few weeks before that women's worship time, I had gone to the altar after a Sunday morning service and told God, "*If You don't do something with this, I can't make it. I can't handle it anymore and I don't know what to do with it. I just know I can't go on like this.*" (You should know that I don't particularly like going to church altars. So, I avoid it, when possible, in favor of "*making my own personal altar at my seat.*" But this time, I hurt so badly that I didn't care. I needed help.)

God being God does all in His own timing. Gradually, He drew me back into Bible Study through my facilitating a bible study group at church. During this time, I also sought out a personal, Christian counselor to talk to. My counselor helped me to unpack life events once I decided to be honest about how AND why I felt the way that I did. (*That was hard!*) As the counselor helped me, God started to reveal to me how several of my relationships in life were indirectly affected by events involving my Dad and how I saw him.

Remember, he represented power in my life; very controlling. In order to get along with him, you had to do things his way. If you didn't you were wrong and stupid. Every decision had to go through him first. And the answer was usually, No. If he was angry with you; you felt like you HAD to walk on eggshells around him until you managed to get into his good graces again. Or, you just didn't deal with him.

I was an adult, married with children and had been out of his house for more than a decade AND he was living in *my* house, but I still didn't want to cross him and sought to appease his anger should it occur. Since

I couldn't treat him the way he HAD treated me, I passive aggressively treated other relationships in my life that way.

I always felt that I knew what direction others should take. After all, I didn't want them to fail or go wrong. I knew I was always right. If they didn't agree with me, I shunned them. If they made me angry, instead of talking about what they had done, I would just distance myself from them, because I hated confrontations.

All of this was an eye opener; courtesy of God, my Father. There was a lot of denial on my part. It's amazing how we tend to actualize the traits we hate in others.

About a year after that women's fellowship morning, I was asked to be a part of another bible study outside of my church. A group was studying Beth Moore's, *'Breaking Free.'*[ii] It was through this study that the revelation came about how my feelings about my dad were affecting me and other relationships of mine.

I had not forgiven him; I had hated him, which was very apparent by the way I talked about him (*Usually only the bad stuff; rarely any good, though, there had been the occasional good time.*) Because I hated him, I was also hating myself. My relationship with myself was two-faced: I could hate him one minute and beat myself up the next for having done so, while asking myself WWJD – "What Would Jesus Do?") I **had** to forgive him and forgive myself. Then wholeheartedly learn to love and appreciate myself. What a very TALL order this was for me!

I could say it didn't take long to achieve this, but I would be lying. I was big on owning my own part in situations, until it was a heavy situation. Owning means seeing **and** understanding the part I played and not putting it all on the other person or the devil. Yes, both of them play a part, but

I had to learn that owning my part does not, in any way, mean the other party gets away with anything. It simply means that if I owned my own behavior then, I must trust God to deal with the behavior of the other parties involved.

In this case, my father has been deceased for more than 20 years. To be clear, I loved my father. And I honored him as the Bible instructed; but I hated how he treated us at times and unfortunately, those times seem to outweigh the good I saw.

I have forgiven him. I've come to understand that brokenness is something all of us have in our DNA. We manifest it differently though. Some brokenness is actually acceptable in society. At least it was for my Dad.

It was just part of our communal fabric. Even though his behavior was terrible at times, no one knew how to help or confront him and everyone chose their own way of dealing with it. I chose mine. As a result, even though there were some good times, they have been overshadowed in my memory by the bad. I've struggled to recall them.

My Heavenly Father patiently waited for me to look to Him for the help I needed to forgive daddy. I needed to connect the link between my feelings for daddy and about myself *and* to see myself as my Heavenly Father saw me. Healing gradually shows itself as I increasingly give more over to Him. I now love myself in ways I had not thought possible. I can accept that this is a process and I enjoy it when I can look back and see how love heals. Praise be to God Who made it all possible! Hate doesn't live here anymore.

Hate doesn't live here anymore.

---

i This resource helped me overcome my hatred and unforgiveness. Though a great resource this in no way is an endorsement for anyone to run out and attend or purchase it. Results may not be the same. Also, no compensation of any kind was received for mentioning it in my story.
ii IBID

Mae Golden is a born-again believer who feels honored to be a wife, mother, god-mother and trusted friend. Spending her early adult years being a military wife and raising her 3 children, she learned how much she loved using her hands to make crafts, bake, sew, garden etc.

Entering the workforce after her children were in school, helped her to realize her love of learning and teaching others, which eventually led her to a master's degree in Instructional Systems Design.

Currently, Mae has two businesses (one is instructional design based and the other is a handmade jewelry business), with aspirations towards third one and she has a blog.

Mae would be the first to say her walk with God has been eventful, exciting and challenging, but she wouldn't change a thing. Constantly amazed by what she learns and unlearns about God, His Love and His Grace towards her, she is thoroughly certain that every action good or bad is still moving her towards and in God's purpose for her life. And for that, she's grateful!

CONNECT WITH ME:
BLOG WEBSITE: Blossomingintopurpose.com
FACEBOOK: Blossoming into Purpose
EMAIL: blossomingintopurpose@gmail.com

CURVY GIRL ACCESSORIES
JEWELRY WEBSITE: curvygirlaccessories.com
INSTAGRAM AND **FACEBOOK**:
curvygirlaccessoriesllc

www.ingramcontent.com/pod-product-compliance
Lightning Source LLC
Chambersburg PA
CBHW071413290426
44108CB00014B/1800